About
Skill Builders
Handwriting

by Clareen Arnold

Welcome to Rainbow Bridge Publishing's Skill Builders series. Like our Summer Bridge Activities collection, the Skill Builders series is designed to make learning fun and rewarding.

The Skill Builders *Traditional Manuscript* handwriting exercises were developed to provide parents and teachers with a tool for reinforcing handwriting skills as children learn to print. Parents should plan on helping their children with these pages.

This book begins with instruction pages for making each of the letters in the Traditional Manuscript style. These include a tracing exercise to give students the chance to shape each letter in its uppercase and lowercase form, followed by space they can use to practice writing the letter on their own. From there, the book moves on to word and sentence formation. There is a practice page for each letter with words that begin with that letter, followed by a practice page for each letter with words that begin with that letter in a sentence.

Learning is more effective when approached with an element of fun and enthusiasm. That's why the Skill Builders combine entertaining and academically sound exercises with engaging graphics and fun themes—to make reviewing basic skills fun and effective, for both you and your budding scholars.

Table of Contents

C C C - - - -

C C C - - - -

c c c - - - -

C C C - - - -

d d d - - - -

D D D - - - -

d d d - - - -

D D D - - - -

Flour

6

MILK

m m m

M M M M

m m m

M M M M

n n n

N N N

n n n

N N N

Traditional Manuscript—RBP3012

W W W

W

W W W

W

X

X

A A A A A

a a a a a

Ann Ann

ant ant

an an

am am

are are

ate ate

air air

Al the alligator
ate an apple.

Al the alligator
ate an apple.

B B

b b

Bob Bob

bus bus

big big

bat bat

bed bed

bird bird

bear bear

Bear bounces
the beach ball.

Bear bounces the
beach ball.

C C C ___ ___

c c ___ ___

Carl Carl ___

car car ___

cat cat ___

cow cow ___

can can ___

cup cup ___

calf calf ___

Cow watches
the crab crawl.

Cow watches
the crab crawl.

D D __ __

d d __ __

Don Don __

day day __

did did __

do do __

dry dry __

dog dog __

duck duck

Dolphin dives
for doughnuts.

Dolphin dives
for doughnuts.

E   E

e   e

Eva Eva

eat eat

each each

eye eye

ear ear

elf elf

eel eel

Ed Elephant sits on an egg.

Ed Elephant sits on an egg.

F F F

f f f

Fred Fred

fan fan

frog frog

fur fur

fig fig

fox fox

fish fish

Find five fat, freckled fish.

Find five fat, freckled fish.

G G

g g

Greg Greg

gas gas

gym gym

get get

go go

gum gum

give give

Giraffe slips on
giant gum balls.
Giraffe slips on
giant gum balls.

H H

h h

Hal Hal

hen hen

ham ham

hog hog

hit hit

hay hay

hat hat

Is Horse hiding
in the hay?

Is Horse hiding
in the hay?

I I — — —

I i — — —

i i — — —

Ike Ike

it it

if if

in in

itch itch

ivy ivy

ice ice

Ike Iguana eats
icky insects.

Ike Iguana eats

icky insects.

J J J J J

j j j j j

Jay Jay

jar jar

job job

jam jam

jail jail

jug jug

jet jet

Jaguar juggles
with jellybeans.

Jaguar juggles
with jellybeans.

K K — — — —

k k — — — —

Kay Kay

kid kid

keep keep

key key

knit knit

keg keg

kite kite

Katie Kangaroo
flies a kite.

Katie Kangaroo
flies a kite.

L

I

Lou Lou

leg leg

let let

lid lid

log log

lips lips

lion lion

Llama laughs at
Lizard's joke.

Llama laughs at
Lizard's joke.

M M

m m

Meg Meg

mad mad

men men

mug mug

mix mix

mop mop

mill mill

Mike Mouse

dances to music.

Mike Mouse

dances to music.

N N _____ _____

n n _____ _____

Nate Nate

nut nut

nap nap

not not

nine nine

net net

nest nest

No nest needs

ninety nuts.

No nest needs

ninety nuts.

O O _ _ _

o o _ _ _

Otis Otis

old old

out out

one one

ox ox

oil oil

owl owl

Ostrich likes to
watch Octopus.

Ostrich likes to
watch Octopus.

P   P   P

p   p   p

Peg   Peg

put   put

pan   pan

pen   pen

pop   pop

play   play

pig   pig

Pink Pig hides
in a pumpkin.
Pink Pig hides
in a pumpkin.

Quinn Quinn

quail quail

quick quick

quiet quiet

quit quit

quest quest

queen queen

Quiet Quail

quilts quickly.

Quiet Quail

quilts quickly.

R R R

r r r

Russ Russ

red red

ran ran

rug rug

rock rock

ride ride

rabbit rabbit

Rooster and Rat

romp in the rain.

Rooster and Rat

romp in the rain.

S S S _ _ _ _

s s s _ _ _ _

Sam Sam

sad sad

sky sky

she she

sun sun

sit sit

seal seal

Snake tells

Skunk a secret.

Snake tells

Skunk a secret.

T I I

t t t

Ted Ted

tag tag

tell tell

ten ten

two two

tub tub

turtle turtle

Tom Tiger took
a trip to Texas.

Tom Tiger took

a trip to Texas.

U U U

u u u

Uma Uma

use use

up up

ugly ugly

ultra ultra

under under

unicorn unicorn

Unicorn is under the umbrella.

Unicorn is under the umbrella.

V V

V v

Vera Vera

very very

voice voice

van van

view view

vase vase

vacuum vacuum

Vulture received

a valentine.

Vulture received

a valentine.

W W W

w w w

Wes Wes

will will

wag wag

web web

wasp wasp

wax wax

wolf wolf

Whale was in
a whirlwind.

Whale was in

a whirlwind.

X X

X X

Xavier Xavier

X-ray X-ray

xylophone
xylophone

xenops xenops

Rex Fox looks
at a xylophone.

Rex Fox looks
at a xylophone.

Y Y

Y y

Yeda Yeda

yell yell

yes yes

you you

yet yet

yeah yeah

yarn yarn

Yak plays with
yellow yarn.

Yak plays with
yellow yarn.

Z Z

Z z

Zeke Zeke

zap zap

zig zig

zag zag

zoom zoom

zebra zebra

zipper zipper

Zookeepers feed
Zebra at the zoo.

Zookeepers feed

Zebra at the zoo.

One One One

Two Two Two

Three Three Three

Four

Five

Six

69

7 7 7

Seven   Seven

8 8 8

Eight   Eight

9 9 9

Nine   Nine

10　10　＿

Ten　Ten　Ten

11　11　＿

Eleven　Eleven

12　12　＿

Twelve　Twelve

Colors

red

yellow

blue

green

black

brown

orange

purple

Shapes

line

oval

star

circle

square

triangle

diamond

rectangle

Food

pizza

soup

beans

milk

eggs

apple

toast

burrito

corn

juice

yogurt

bread

cereal

meat

cheese

nuts

peas

Traditional Manuscript—RBP3012

January

February

March
April
May
June
July

August

September

October

November

December

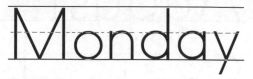
Monday

Tuesday

Wednesday

Thursday

Friday

Saturday

Sunday

week

month

year

birthday

night

day

minute

hour

noon

morning

afternoon

evening